Dr Carla Davis

How To Be A Better Wife

Top (5) Five Secret To Having An Amazing Relationship With Your Husband

First edition

This book was professionally typeset on Reedsy
Find out more at reedsy.com

Contents

1. Who Is The Perfect Wife..1
2. What Qualities Make A Great Wife..............................4
3. What Wives Should Do 13
4. How Do I Please My Husband 22
5. Advice For A Wife...27

    1.

    2.

    3.

    4.

1

Who Is The Perfect Wife

Ladies are often named either a "decent partner" or a "hunky partner" which makes me question: what's the meaning of a very decent life partner? Who is she? What are the boundaries to survey assuming that the lady is good or terrible?

It truly does now at this point not come as a marvel that a glance through the web will intentionally be many sites looking at being an incredibly decent wife. In any case, the man eccentric culture has previously concluded what makes a woman a "pleasant partner". Their meaning of being a very decent partner strategies a woman being trained and pleasantly knowledgeable with own circle of family members errands, who needs to be quiet and is handiest fixated on taking care of the house and isn't generally striking, one who knows how to make changes for her own circle of family members' joy. An extreme character who doesn't have an unmistakable overflow of energy!

Cutting-region ladies can likewise moreover challenge what makes a fantastic wife. Consequently, it very well may be inappropriate to guess that a phenomenal wife suits the cliche picture of an incredibly decent young lady. As a substitute, there are different strategies to make a wedding a triumph, but it's miles handiest plausible on the off chance that every occasion is learned to picture.

Marriage changes the existence of a woman; from a spoiled lighthearted young lady, she develops legitimate freedoms into a responsible wife coordinated to assume the commitments of a wife. Indeed, even as people offer breathtaking kinds of counsel on marriage, the remarkable elements of a top notch wife are standard.

There are excellent patterns pretty much every person looks for within the woman with whom he needs to unwind and develop a fate. In any case, marriage requires each ally to be dedicated to make it a solid dating.

The Ideal Wife

he woman who knows about the method for controlling herself from bedding space to lounge to kitchen to working environment lodge to show room with a similar artfulness and flashiness.

One who knows about her significant other higher than he personally does.

She, who can control any fiasco in a matter of seconds, fixes and resolves the issues sooner than they push up.

She knows about the method for saving the funds.

The individual who keeps a grin on her and her significant other's face regardless of what the situation is.

She is aware of the way to win her person's coronary heart regardless of his life structures.

A phenomenal life partner gets fine and changes a person. She directs him to the right course and stands through him through thick and thin. She takes care of the children and deals with the aggregate at home, practically independently. She is a multitask er who oversees canvases and homegrown with accuracy.

A gigantic spouse ought not be discourteous nearer to her significant other non-public region in the marriage. Anybody objectives a bit of 'personal time' thus, attacking that non-public area should be something a fantastic wife should not in the slightest bit do.

One of the most helpful ways to be a decent wife is to be liberal towards your significant other and his necessities. You can convey this liberality in your caring words, obliging activities, and understanding responses towards any error that your significant other makes. Benevolence towards your husband will cause them to feel adored and upheld. In any event, when you can't help contradicting them, your liberality will help your better half not feel cornered and focused on. A liberal demeanor is an extraordinary spot to begin correspondence with your accomplice.

Address the issues

Battles could appear to be horrendous and quite serene, yet this isn't correct. Quietness can be a method for denying or staying away from an issue that may be significant for the sound working of a relationship.

Each battle in a marriage does not merit having. A critical illustration to realize while attempting to comprehend how to be a decent wife is to relinquish the minor things that irritate you.

Minor issues continue to come up in relationships, and on the off chance that you continue to have quarrels over them, the relationship will continually be in a condition of contention and strain. Practice persistence and motivation to conclude which issues merit having a contention over.

Keep things hot

In finding out about how to be a decent wife, remember about sex and keeping things fiery.

Notice your better half and attempt to comprehend what a spouse needs from his significant other in the room. You can propose new things and keep a receptive outlook to stay away from sex from becoming exhausting or drawn-out for you or your significant other.

2

What Qualities Make A Great Wife

An incredible wife first loves herself.

At the point when you love yourself, you manage yourself. This way you do all that to keep yourself engaged by changing your external clothing types, by ensuring your hair is prepared, cosmetics, cleanliness, garments, and so on are completely assembled. Practice and healthy weight are imperative.

For some men, finding a decent wife is a visually impaired person's buff, because of the reality that they don't perceive the characteristics of an astounding wife to post for. It is indispensable to say that understanding the characteristics of a decent wife will direct your pursuit while you are ready to get one.

Most folks are particularly motivated by what they see. How one presents themselves is fundamental. Notwithstanding, as we all perceive, that substantial comprehensive bundle isn't the entire part. Character is in a manner of significance. Being an extraordinary wife is checking out your mentality. What do you seem like? How is your tone? How would you respond to your husband once they aren't doing what you'd like?

What's your energy? Is your husband repulsed by having sex with you or would they say they are drawn to you? Do you understand a method for chuckling, being a tease, being smooth anyway, shrewd in getting what you really want?

Do you offer commendations to your man, consolation, solace, compassion, and love? Or on the other hand do you make him need to want to change into another person altogether?

Is it true or not that you are unconstrained? Daring? Fun? Or on the other hand would you say you are unsurprising? Customary? Losing bid? When did you last flabbergast your person with passes to a game? Sex inside the car back sit? A wonder to go to work? A current card to his favored store? When did you last think to give him an affection letter, maybe in any event, consisting of an enchanting picture, a dash of fragrance, and a sign of where to find you?

What do you spend your time doing together? Do you play prepackaged games, watch motion pictures, exit to eat, take off on his return, snare him with the water hose in a swimsuit simultaneously as he's out of entryways working on something? Could you at any point be learning with him? Could you at any point cry and extend your deepest sentiments? Could you at any point illuminate him should you be held? Could you at any point murmur in his ear? Could you at any point cause him to seem fantastic before his companions, around family members, associates, and so on?

Are good at giving without needing anything in return, or is it all one good turn deserves another? Will you presently at this point not be a sucker? Could you at any point help him? Could you at any point win him together alongside your delicate quality and generosity in inclination to cruel and danger? When he's done wrong, would you say you are ready to precisely portray him in affection, in private (presently at this point not before the children)?

Could you at any point keep on grinning at him? Is it true that you are guaranteed in yourself or generally discouraged and setting yourself down? Do you lash out effectively or would you say you are steady to outrage and brief to excuse? Could you at any point settle or would you say you are fragile? Do you have any desires, leisure activities, yearnings, dreams, objectives? Could you at any point fill in the holes where the individual wishes to help or is feeble?

Ladies with qualities of a great wife are valuable and are managers, and that they merit the entirety of the consideration and esteem because of the reality that they've the most perfect expectations for the house.

One of the reasons why a female is labeled a great wife is because of her preparation to make the wedding work. At the point when the couple deviates, an extraordinary life partner could notice the lead of her significant other and be open to settling issues genially.

Additionally, an astounding wife realizes her significant other can not be great, so she no longer fights to form him into her optimal model. Rather, she changes with his persona and remedies his weaknesses while he blunders. Which furthermore permits her to embrace herself as an amazing individual

Here are 20 attributes of a great wife:

1. Mindful and merciful

An astounding wife is popular for her consideration and sympathy. She is sensitive to her own circle of family members' desires, and does her high-good to offer an answer. She knows when her better half is baffled, and endeavors to satisfy him.

Her being concerned attitude makes her own circle of family members not lacking in any component of ways of life.

2. Touchy of the little matters

An amazing wife isn't unaware of the little matters that happen inside her home.

For example, assuming her husband does something viewed as little, she no longer overlooks it. Rather, she heats up affectionately and values him. Then again, assuming that the husband is troubled about something within the house, she makes an honest effort to reestablish it.

3. Hangs out alongside her better half

Young Couple in an affection manner sitting in a Pr-winter Park Resting Up against a Tree Embracing Each other

Regardless of how occupied the coolest partner's time table is, she makes time to spend along with her better half.

A few women don't invest energy with their spouses utilizing pardons like an extremely active time table. An incredible wife realizes that the extraordinary time spent proceeds with the flash inside the marriage.

4. Empowers her better half

One crucial capability of a partner in a person's way of life is proceeding as a stockpile of consolation and direction.

In each great and horrendous time, one of the qualities of an ideal wife is to motivate and show to her better half that he's cherished. At the point when men revel in difficult situations, they don't see their worth.

In any case, an extraordinary wife helps them to remember the splendid, all around certainly worth they have.

5. Regards her better half

An effective marriage prospers in reverence. In the event that you're attempting to track down the qualities of an extraordinary life partner, guarantee she is deferential.

Furthermore, an astounding wife values her better half's work, and the husband responds with appreciation and love.

6. Puts her family first

Assuming you're considering what to look for in a life partner, perceive that a decent wife puts her own family members first.

The family' needs and needs apex her needs, and the person in question is presently at this point not remorseful about it. An amazing wife will go the more noteworthy mile to ensure her home life is cushy for her significant other and kids.

7. Husband's high-agreeable buddy and sweetheart

An amazing wife doesn't cheat because of the reality that her significant other is her solitary sweetheart.

Furthermore, even though she has other friends, she knows that her better half is her best est buddy. On the off chance that there are any forthcoming issues, she talks first to her significant other, who duplicates as best bud.

8. A brilliant issue solver

In marriage, one of the qualities of an extraordinary wife to look for is her readiness and ability to resolve issues.

An amazing wife neither passes on each of the issues to her significant other to determine. All things considered, she works on the whole along with her better half to battle those issues. And provide means of settling those issues.

9. Treasures cooperation

What makes a great wife is her potential to team up and partake as an energetic cooperative person. She doesn't permit or pass on her significant other to deal with issues all alone, on the grounds that they are both in it together.

Rather, she contributes her standard, she perceives her significant other's work. An amazing wife knows that cooperative endeavors hold the marriage unblemished as the entire part is going without a hitch.

10. Doesn't encroach on her significant other's confidential space

An amazing wife realizes that everyone wants their confidential space.

At the point when she sees her significant other wishes for an alone time, she regards his choice. She is moreover visionary as she knows about the appropriate opportunity to warm up as much to her significant other and encourage him.

11. She is heartfelt

Couple Embracing Together on an ocean side with the sun above them

At the point when it includes sentiment, an ideal wife knows about a method for joining this into her marriage.

She is direct and does little matters that trap her significant other ignorant. She is tricky to her better half's desires, and uses this to make heartfelt motions.

12. She evades misrepresentation

An amazing wife is typically genuine to herself and her words. She isn't a copycat.

Despite the fact that she has coaches and capable models from whom she learns from, she remains legitimate and her genuine self because of the way that it is what points to her significant other and her marriage.

13. Imparts actually

Being an extraordinary life partner requires the focal point of strong verbal trade.

At the point when there are issues inside the marriage, she endeavors to hold an open verbal trade in inclination to being quiet about them. She keeps her better half from speculating as she lays bare her contemplation and proffers techniques to move forward.

14. Draws out the best in her better half

One of the imperative attributes of an amazing wife is her capability to ensure her significant other accomplishes his most noteworthy potential.

She gives her better half the devotion and direction he wishes to survive. She knows about how compelling her job is inside her family, and she utilizes it to her better half and in her home.

15. She offers a listening ear

One of the improvements of being an ideal wife is the possibility to offer a listening ear because of the reality she knows that it helps in strong verbal trade.

Consequently, in inclination to just hearing, she pays attention to perceive her significant other. At the point when her better half demands to discuss being alone with her, she proceeds with all interruptions under control to perceive him.

16. Commends her significant other's prosperity

One of the characteristics of a great wife is she doesn't consider her significant other's prosperity to be a method for contending. Rather, she values him and perceives his endeavors.

In the event that there are children, she holds onto the likelihood to apply her better half's accomplishments to motivate them.

17. She is earnest

A man can concur with his wife while she has ended up being genuine vast times.

Enduring relationships are built on genuineness and strong verbal trade. There's a turn to being earnest; you don't need to obviously make reference to something. For example, on the off chance that you could do without his footwear, you might change them with the guide of getting new coordinates.

18. Imaginative in bed

For the most part, men love women who're superb in bed as well as the other way around.

Truth be told, for a couple of men, it's far one of the imperative qualities of an extraordinary wife in a relationship. A fantastic female does concentrate en route to satisfy her better half's in bed. Along these lines, he doesn't look outside.

On the off chance that her significant other loves a definite intercourse style, she aces it and offers him the best in bed.

19. Her non common ways of life is zenith indent

An amazing wife takes her non mainstream ways of life altogether because of the reality she knows that it's undeniably more helpful to her significant other and home. She petitions God for her better half and family, and the person reflects routinely.

Additionally, she promises her better half is doing appropriately in a profound sense as it permits them to bond higher in confidence.

20. Stays excellent for her better half and home

At the point when matters are looking through hopelessly inside the home, a great wife knows that she needs to save an excellent outlook for the environment to remain cool.

Notwithstanding the downside, she proceeds with the house in superb structure regardless of whether it's far disappointing.

Most importantly, one of the characteristics of an amazing wife is understanding that her home should be a protected area for her own family to develop, play and live.

Thus, she is unrelenting in achieving this.

At the point when you spot a female you like,review reasonable discussions around those qualities of an ideal wife to offer a discernment into the kind of character she is.

3

What Wives Should Do

Despite the fact that I've been hitched for a couple of years at this point, I genuinely should recall my better half's cravings. I should ponder the potential aftereffects of my reckless words, perspectives, and moves, less I ruin his mind-sets and how he sees me.

What are those things a wife shouldn't have or do in her marriage?

I requested a number of comments from my wedded companions, "What should a wife forestall doing on the off chance that she wants to upgrade her marriage?" The list is fundamentally founded absolutely on their reactions.

1. Try not to put others first before your better half.
God planned friendship in marriage altogether so that a couple can meet each other for a nearby, personal, human dating. He even expressed in Genesis 2:18, "It isn't generally reasonable for a man to be all alone, I will make a suitable companion for him."

So what happens while you place your mother, a friend's necessities before your significant other's? In reality, you're making a stride (much of the time unexpected) towards seclusion for your marriage. In the event that you decide, for instance, to go through a day shopping along with your mom while your significant other mentioned you to cook for him, it basically implies his sentiments are not substantial nor esteemed, and he is not respected.

2. Never use intercourse to make an arrangement or as a vengeance gadget.
A few women purposely or coincidentally share with their husband, "When I get what I want, you get intercourse."

A wife isn't to deny her significant other sex because of the reality the individual is the zenith of the family, and his feelings should not be played with, no matter what. sex is close to home and concretes a superior relationship .

Sex make an association among individuals concerned, uniquely in a marriage, and that it means a lot to manage marriage as consecrated. Thus, women must not torment their spouses through methods of refusal.

Sex should not be utilized as a gadget for retribution in the event of doubt among the couple because of the reality it's extremely dangerous to marriage and should be stayed away from; the young lady should devise various techniques to call for interest from her significant other.

There isn't any support for the couples to apply intercourse as torment to cure their disparities.

3.Stop reminding your better half over past issues
Try not to cause him to appear to be less capable or criticize him about little stuff. One companion expressed that once we persistently remind our significant other's about minor stuff like eating regimen, weight, medicine, picking when to launder, and so forth. We are most certainly showing up more like his mother than his significant other.

4.prevent dealing with your significant other like he's a child.

This might hit a nerve with various women, but it happens all too much of the time. I, at the end of the day, have done this multiple times. Also, I came to acknowledge I was off-base. While trying to bring out the "pleasant" in our husbands, we start mothering them. In the event that we want to draw out the thoughtfulness in our significant other, we need to show him that we Regard him regardless of whether he presently does not deserve it yet.

I comprehend this seems insane, but almost every marriage digital book I really have at any point contemplates underscores the spouse's striking need for reverence from his significant other. We should show to him that we appreciate him and notice what happens. Simply see how he adapts to the situation. As for the better parts, we have novel abilities regarding the matter of this. A husband wants his better half, not another mother.

5.We ought to Express whatever we might be thinking and forestall depending on our non-verbal correspondence.

Most women I know (myself included) fight with this. We by and large will generally havereasonable instinct, so we depend on our significant other too. The amusing and aggravating issue is that nine times out of 10, they just take our word for it. They aren't concentrating on our body language, moans, or eye rolls. This transforms into a Gigantic difficulty while we consistently depend on our non-verbals to do all the "speak-me".

Non-verbals should essentially decorate our words, instead of being our goals. As married women, we ought to have the option to pull away from "speak-me"matters... and use WORDS. More words implies real understanding. We should give our spouses love and in actuality give our hearts to them. Closeness gets advanced with connection.

6.We ought to prevent flirting with different men.

This one likely looks as though it's an easy decision to the limit of you,however it's a Major issue in loads of relationships. It could likewise furthermore start when you begin giggling and making coy jokes with another man. Then, at that point, you go for lunch simply you two. Before you understand it, the messages start coming. Then, texts and calls. Also, then, that man is all you might ponder. You begin concealing any correspondence with this man from your significant other. Before you understand it, you wind up in a sexual undertaking.

"How did I arrive?"...

"How did I permit it to get this far?", you think.

He's simply a man you cherished addressing at work.

It was only a couple of innocuous teases, correct?

Friends, we ought to wake up to reality. Not being a tease out of the entryways of our marriage is reasonable. "Innocently being a tease can't actually exist". It is the doorway to extramarital undertakings, and it might wreck relationships.

As married ladies, we can most likely have discussions with various men in the workplace, church, or outside, but we don't have to play with those various men. We should give our all to not be all alone with some other person that isn't our significant other or close family member. No good thing can emerge out of it.

At the point when we address different guys,in a few certain ways that appear to be an open invitation to befriend you, do we stop to have considerations like "would I feel awful assuming my better half is having this equivalent verbal trade (that I am having) with another young lady?". In the event that the response is "Yes" we're beyond the field of play, and we ought to stop the verbal trade right away. This could likewise moreover sound exuberant, but it basically may save your marriage.

At the point when we play with fire, we should expect to get burned. We should do all that we can to watch and safeguard our relationships.

7.Tarnishing his picture in the children's presence.
At the point when a husband isn't generally beyond a shadow of a doubt doing his obligations at home, many wives make it a component of commitment to make their husbands bad to their children. They obliterate his picture in the kind of way that the children will flip their lower back on him. This is underhandedness. Regardless of how dreadful an individual could have all the earmarks of being, they'll consistently be a particle of goodness in him and obliterating his picture could likewise furthermore have repercussions.

8.Don't cause your better half to gain your appreciation.

Similarly as a husband needs to genuinely cherish his significant other, a wife needs to regard her better half genuinely. That doesn't suggest that she needs to like all that he does or acknowledge all he says as reality. Furthermore, it doesn't suggest that she ought to adapt to insignificant lead or developments from him. However, it suggests, paying little mind to what he does or says, she needs to manage him with nobility and distinction because of the reality he's her significant other.

9. Quit Being So Serious constantly

Being an adult is so intense. There are times where I basically keep myself from lamenting how extreme being a grown-up is. For that reason we believe our husbands should give tomfoolery and joy into our lives!

Nobody wishes to be excessively serious, so every once in a while, allow yourself and your significant other an opportunity to live and appreciate life. Try not to worry about straightforward issues, let things go.

For reasons unknown, numerous men are fit for typifying a touch extra easily than women. So why not quit forestalling to oppose laughing at their dumb jokes and encapsulate the happiness they offer that would be useful

Life is basically excessively short for it to all be work and in no way, shape or form be play!

Embrace tomfoolery and make time to laugh together, plan a night out, or play an entertainment together! Have some time off from being an adult and experience being with the main individual you love. This will assist with raising the tension loads of us are wearing and as well as reinforcing the bond which you have together alongside your better half.

10.Stop Making Arrangements without the Contribution of Your Significant other

In the event that we want our husbands to be our legitimate sidekicks, we ought to start including them with the data of ourdays. The fact of the matter is while we forestall asking our husband for his feedback, they forestall needing to have a say.

Most women will settle on choices without their husbands' information . In any case, an urgent part to not neglect is that marriage is a cooperation.

Deciding to rest on somebody doesn't infer that you're unequipped for accomplishing something all alone, but rather it is vital to do things together. Only because of the reality we're able to thoroughly keep up with the issues of our homes alone doesn't infer we need to.

At the point when we start exploring every last bit of it all alone, our relationships ordinarily begin to endure.

Marriage is the approaching of two lives transforming into one.

We ought to be deliberate about sharing our choices creating processes with one another altogether, so that our association can flourish and eventually so our security can hold to develop.

11.Stop Dealing with Your Significant other Like He Is Futile

The women I know are loaded with power, knowledge, and freedom. We are rock-in' rollers!

These are incredible attributes that one can't change out of. Nonetheless, they ought to be exposed in a good way. In the event that we aren't wary, we force the possibility of railroading our spouses appropriately to leave our homes and relationships.

God knows this about women and for that reason he trains us to move toward our spouses with accommodation and regard (Ephesians 5:22-23). God made a female to be the E'er-partner; this means to help, deliverer, hero, or defender. We arrived at the scene from the beginning with a reason!

Our goal is to be the assistant, get the undertaking executed, God realizes that along with our energy, might be a power that might make it extreme for us to delay and consider that our husbands could likewise furthermore have something to give as well.

I perceive firsthand that fighting is genuine. Numerous men see issues in one more manner than numerous ladies. They regularly are dwelling second to second while simultaneously as we tend to interface the dabs and typically work to be all assembled for what's in store.

It's OK on the off chance that we view our disparities as an obstruction to us working appropriately together, but truly, we need each other's disparities to carry on within our lives appropriately. We each have qualities and shortcomings that the other can praise.

Essentially, this dynamic could likewise give off an impression of us sorting out our children' need to rest at a specific time while simultaneously as our husbands are fascinated in something different as opposed to making it lights-out time for the kid, while we are occupied with cooking. Our Mom's impulses can jump out in a way that conveys irreverence to our significant other.

We could likewise furthermore begin to push toward a short response while not giving what we need. Attempting to get what we need doesn't give us a permit to disregard, slight, or belittle our accessory.

We wedded them because of the reality we want to consider their viewpoint. We ought to be careful to never again allow our "rightness" in our brains to flip us into hard individuals.

12.Having Ridiculous Assumptions

Searching an excess of assumptions out of your significant other and afterward being miserable about it, since he didn't gettogether with you, will rapidly wreck your marriage. Assuming that you experience misery, first review reality. Anticipating that your husband should make you fulfilled is unreasonable. You can best make yourself fulfilled.

Most women have different friends, who fill various jobs. We have a friend with whom we enjoy shopping with. One friend loves to exercise with us. One friend drives a book of scriptures study. One friend likes to have coffee on Wednesday mornings.

Each man or lady in your life satisfies a particular and significant job. None is extra urgent; they're just unambiguous. Assuming you expect your significant other to be great and bring you never-ending bliss, never again are you putting him up for disappointment, but you likewise are setting yourself up for dissatisfaction.

Endeavor to build your circle of impact, to comprise of many individuals, who fill your ways of life with explicit endowments. Track down the expense and gain of every companionship to explicit areas of your ways of life.

In particular, track down ways of encountering the entire parcel and be happy with who you're as a lady. Look to find your own satisfaction, inside yourself.

13.Criticizing, Putting down, and Ridiculing Him to Your Loved ones

At the point when you condemn and disparage your better ha**lf, you never again respect your significant other in your own eyes**, but you besides could harm the ones nearest to you. You pressure them to favor one side, and the course. They pick your side, because in reality they should be trustworthy of you. Your friends and your own family don't live at your home. They fail to understand what is happening for a large number of days. They don't see the incredible things your significant other does. The best view they've of your significant other is the only one you give them. In the event that you're ceaselessly horrendous mouthing and disparaging him, they might see him as a horrible partner for you.

After you talk gravely about your significant other, your loved ones will in no way, shape or form respect your better half with deference once more. Indeed, even while you recuperate from your outburst, and all is well at home, they may regardless be frantic at him. Your loved ones need to guard you from risk and mischief. On the off chance that you're persistently with respect to your significant other in a horrible light, they might have to safeguard you and your children from this beast you wedded, despite the fact that he isn't genuinely a beast.

At the point when you criticize your significant other, your companionship and connections will keep on being hopelessly changed towards your better half. In time, this might wreck your marriage. He will in no way, shape or form capture why your companions could do without him, and why your family members are cold towards him.

Instead of looking to rationalize, don't start down that way. At the point when you talk about your significant other, use elevating, empowering words. If there is a chance that he's performing like a jerk, you don't need to spout about it to everyone you perceive. Your ordinary legal disputes towards him will make a wall among your significant other and your companions, which he can in no way, shape or form survive.

When that matters are intense at home for a season, you shouldn't impart it to everyone you perceive. You shouldn't likewise illuminate your entire relatives or family members about every contention.

Attempt to talk appropriately of your better half and your relationship. Search for the viable and increase the issues which are working for you.

4

How Do I Please My Husband

Knowing how to satisfy your better half can ponder in your relationship. Shared regard and care are fundamental for sound connections.

Connections are wonderful when the couples please each other with similar methodologies. For instance, you might drive him to grin when he is mad.

You might satisfy him by doing basic things like appearing warm and offering praise. Being a decent audience and communicating your sentiments and feelings can likewise dazzle him. They likewise love the help and support from their wives. In any case, you might recollect that satisfying doesn't imply that you affront or corrupt yourself.

We have seen connections and relationships that have gone bad en route. One strong explanation is that the inclination was one individual was accomplishing a greater amount of giving than getting. Few partners are at fault for getting all the adoration and fondness yet not knowing how to respond.

Certain individuals can appear to be too unbending in some cases. It takes their partners the right chance to turn on the gentlest piece of their heart and keep it on.

There could be a few reasons that can make a marriage disintegrate. Be that as it may, one of the clearest reasons is absence of appreciation.

Should the chance arise that you are anticipating reigniting the flash in your marriage, you should make it a custom to satisfy your life partner.

All in all, would you say you are thinking about how to satisfy your better half?

1.Make home a heaven

Home is supposed to be your significant other's paradise. The rest of the world can be unpleasant to him on occasion. Whenever he is furious, he might need some harmony and alleviation. Make your home a tranquil spot where he can quiet his psyche.

Knowing how to satisfy your better half aides cultivate your bond. Being loving, showering praises, utilizing the force of a touch, and examining dreams are probably the most ideal ways to satisfy your man. Communicating your feelings and evaluating ways of keeping the flash in the relationship, like going on a get-away together, is expected to keep life energizing. It is likewise really smart to design a date and invest some energy sharing the most valuable recollections from an earlier time. Then again, great correspondence, straightforwardness, and giving individual space can assist with keeping away from clashes. It is additionally significant not to make a special effort and hurt your self esteem to satisfy your accomplice.

2.Value Him

The facts confirm that you love your man and regard him, yet is he aware? Does he feel important?

Valuing your man with specific motions like a back rub, rub, a bunch of roses, or even an unexpected outing will cause your man to feel exceptional and furthermore make you indispensable. Show appreciation for anything he does, regardless of how little.

This will lift his pride and confidence and cause him to feel fit for really focusing on you.

3.Be warm

Actual closeness is significant, however men additionally long for some warmth. Attempt a better approach to cause him to feel warm. Send him an astounding adoration letter, hold his hands, or simply say sorry when he is irate or you had a spat. Little motions can never turn out badly. You might in fact get coy and frighten him with an unexpected kiss, or give him a shoulder or back knead.

Give him embraces or kisses without anticipating that it should prompt sex. A little kiss when you both return home from work or a light touch on the arm when he's close by are extraordinary updates that you're here, and that you love him. Have a go at starting little occurrences of actual touch over the course of the day to make him ponder you later on

4.Discuss dreams

Men might be reluctant to be open about their dreams. You can make him share his assumptions, minds, or dreams by utilizing some profound ice breakers and let him in if you are paying attention. When you and your life partner know one another assumptions, it turns out to be not difficult to accomplish them.

5.Be brief in your activities

You can't necessarily design and execute things purposefully — it might turn dull with time. Flabbergast your significant other by being unconstrained in your activities. Emerge from your usual range of familiarity, and accomplish something that your partner would cherish. It very well may be going for a lengthy drive at 12 PM, kissing him when he spruces up, taking a dip together, or arranging an end of the week escape to his #1 area. You might in fact make him confused by luring him on a relaxed day.

6.Plan something fun and unconstrained that both of you have never done.

This will get some dopamine streaming for the both of you, and it's an extraordinary method for showing him that you love and care about him. Evaluate another eatery, do another action together, or disappear for the end of the week to another town. A little novelty in your relationship can't do any harm, and it could make him reconsider you in a sexual manner.

You might advise him to simply get in the vehicle, then drive him to an unexpected area

7. Appreciate his efforts

At the point when you notice he's accomplishing something well, enlighten him. A ton of times, we stall out on a daily schedule to possibly let our husbands know when they mess up, which doesn't leave a ton of space for closeness. To get your significant other contemplating you the entire day, give a shot at a call complimenting something great that he does, and tell him the amount you value him.

For example, assuming he did more tasks than expected that day, you could say, "The house looks so great, honey! Thanks for dealing with that multitude of tasks, you truly blew it out of the recreation area today."

Or on the other hand, on the off chance that he's had an intense week at work, you could say, "You're excelling in work, even with all your additional obligations. I know it's unpleasant, however there is no doubt about it."

8.Be appealing for him.

I'm not discussing the way in which a lady searches in a two-piece, three children later, albeit dealing with oneself genuinely means quite a bit to husbands. The fascination I discuss that a full grown man wants, goes past the physical and into the close to home. At the point when he associates with her at her best, sparkles fly. That implies a lady's adoration for self, her enthusiasm forever, and how she conducts herself will rise above his affection for you. As you typify your appeal, he will mirror that equivalent enthusiasm. A lady who needs a developed man will put resources into carrying on with life to its fullest.

Presently, pose yourself this basic inquiry, "How am I satisfying my man?"

Assuming you end up ailing in any of the properties above, you may not be satisfying your significant other. It means quite a bit to enliven your home with a portion of these stunts to satisfy your man. Allow him to see you distinctively and love you more.

Men should be shown fondness. They additionally need to feel helpless here and there. Thus, don't be excessively unbending with your man.

Satisfy him, regardless of whether it implies leaving your usual range of familiarity. In the event that you don't have any idea how to satisfy your significant other, he could begin pulling endlessly.

5

Advice For A Wife

What are the standards for a really cheerful marriage? There aren't any, truly. More like rules. Since what works for one couple may be dismissed by another. Everything depends. One thing remains, in any case: couples should understand what works for themselves and be purposeful about getting rid of the persistent vices that can sink their relationship. Since the most joyful relationships are upset constantly. They require ease, correspondence, advancement, interest, and an understanding from the couples to continually accomplish the work to help it adjust and prosper. All things considered, there are things that all couples ought to focus on, about contentions, negative behavior patterns, remaining adaptable, and then some.

This marriage guidance from different hitched couples is a decent spot to begin:

1.Give yourself consent to rest on your spouse

Obviously you can deal with yourself, yet a decent aspect regarding being hitched is that you don't need to bear life completely all alone. Allow your mate to deal with you now and again.

2.Take consideration of yourself

"It's not difficult to lose yourself in a marriage," my mother told me. "It's not difficult to support your better half and your relationship and disregard sustaining yourself. Get some much needed rest to reset, and your marriage will be better for it."

3.You don't need to tackle everyone's problem

Be delayed to say, "Gracious, I can assist with that!" And don't feel committed to having an answer for all of your significant other's concerns.

4.You will see a great deal of grotesqueness in your life

Things that you truly do however never make implications of, when you are in a marriage your life partner sees everything. Try not to run from it or deny it; embrace the endowment of having the option to see your wrongdoing all the more plainly as well as the adoration for God through your life partner.

5.Leave your weaknesses at the marriage alter

He picked you. You're sufficient. Try not to attempt to intrigue him. He likely won't be intrigued by the things you're dazzled with about yourself. He picked you and not someone else.

6.Assume the best of one another

Whatever occurs, it's vital to comprehend that your husband most likely had the best aims. To accept it embarrasses you and me, yes. In any case, it's important to keep up with the supposition that your husband; anyway imperfect and aggravating they appear on occasion, had the best outcomes as a primary concern, regardless of the outcome. "In the event that you accept your husband is giving their all, it is doubtful there will be fault and disillusionment". Furthermore, there will be a functioning commitment to determine issues as they emerge since you know you both have each other's well being as a primary concern. Keep in mind "your best" doesn't mean flawlessness – it implies you're giving the circumstance all that you can at that point.

7.Be ready to learn and develop

Everybody messes up, expresses moronic things, misunderstands stuff. Everything without a doubt revolves around how individuals respond that characterizes a relationship. "On the chance that we will gain from our mix-ups as they connect with our husband's requirements and wants, we will flourish – by and by, and in the relationship."

The eagerness to concede botches, and apologize earnestly, is a significant key in making a more profound bond with our accomplice. Thus, swallow that pride and burp out an "Please accept my apologies" the following time you commit an error.

8.Stop fixating on who wins a contention

The urgent want to be correct can be unbelievably disastrous in a relationship, it is nearly as a type of viciousness. The need makes dread and hatred among couples and will ultimately wear the relationship out over the long haul. At the point when couples regard one another, they can acknowledge not being right for keeping a good arrangement.

Fruitful couples know how to pick their fights realizing that closeness implies more than being right on occasion.

This certifies that it isn't vital to chip away at the relationship you have with yourself. as such: You likewise need to take care of yourself. That implies practicing consistently, eating great, and getting sufficient rest. In any event, making normal specialist and dental specialist arrangements is significant. By putting resources into yourself and your own prosperity, it shows your husband that you need to be at your best for them.

9.Be patient with your significant other

You should be adaptable in a marriage. You really want to grasp that, assuming you and your husband genuinely love one another, you're not purposely attempting to make things troublesome. However, definitely, there will come times when you can't concur. In those times, you want to recall that you both are just human. We used to lash out with one another, and afterward beat ourselves up quite seriously in light of the fact that we'd think, 'I ought to be better at this.

10.Never let a day go by without talking

Regardless of whether it's simply a welcome towards the beginning of the day, or a goodnight before bed. Or on the other hand a text or email to say hello. Never let a day go by that you don't converse with your mate. As far as I might be concerned, even on our most exceedingly terrible days, hearing my significant other's voice is a consolation. I realize he feels the same way. We might not have any desire to address one another, yet we realize that we're actually dedicated to one another, and we'll move beyond anything that spat we're confronting. For the two of us, quiet isn't a choice. Also, therefore, we track down our direction back to one another without fail.

11.Choose your pressure

This is extraordinary marriage guidance and, truly, incredible life counsel. You can unfortunately deal with a limited amount a lot of pressure in one day, as an individual and as a component of a family. As we've both aged, we've understood that we're more fit for picking what we need to worry about, and that is our specialty.

What could have appeared to be an enormous arrangement quite a while back — an irritating neighbor, or surprising vehicle inconvenience, for instance — has truly been placed into viewpoint by all we've traversed together. On the chance that you can acknowledge that you'll have stressors in your day to day existence, you can prepare yourself to conclude which ones you'll let influence you and your marriage. Furthermore, more critically, which ones you will not.

12.Be remarkable

Be an interesting jewel for your significant other. You don't have to have excellent actual magnificence. Simply have individual characteristics that are elusive in ladies or even in all mankind, like trustworthiness, empathy, modesty, unwavering, and consistency. At the point when you have these significant characteristics, you won't just be a superior wife yet additionally be the best wife for your better half.

13.Be simpler to trust

Your significant other may adore you genuinely and profoundly, and he will trust you consistently. In any case, assuming that he generally discovers you lying and breaking your commitments, he will battle to trust you. Be a superior wife by continuously rehearsing trustworthiness. Demonstrate to your significant other that you can be relied upon. Love your better half consequently by making it simple for him to trust you.

14.Be a liberal and benevolent wife.

Quit keeping track of who's winning in your relationship. Stop griping since you offer more than whatever your better half contributes. Indeed, you reserve the privilege to dissent, however isn't love about offering without expecting that your husband will likewise give something as a trade off?

To be a better wife, you must be liberal, and that implies giving with a happy heart. Furthermore, did you realize the contrast among gifts and elegance? A gift is something you get in light of the fact that you work for itself and you merit it. Then again, elegance is something you get regardless of whether you merit it.

Be a thoughtful wife by cherishing your significant other regardless of whether at times he doesn't merit it.

15.Have insight

Figure out how to go with better choices for your loved ones. Comprehend how to perceive right from wrong. Work on your insight and skill to commit less missteps. On the chance that you become smarter, your significant other would have less issues.

Toward the end of the day's end, the main thing I gained from various accounts of hitched individuals is that, What works for another person may not work for you. Accept notice of the exhortation and direction of your loved ones and trust, then develop your own way. You're responsible for your own joyfully ever later.

At long last, being an amazing wife doesn't just change you into a better wife, yet it likewise helps you reawaken overall new and a better individual.